SUMMARY

of

Jocko Willink & Leif Babin's

THE

DICHOTOMY

OF

LEADERSHIP

Balancing the Challenges of Extreme Ownership

BY

CHRIS LAMBERTSEN

Summary of *The Dichotomy of Leadership:*
Balancing the Challenges of Extreme Ownership
by Jocko Willink and Leif Babin

Paperback ISBN: 978-0-9898229-7-8
Also available as an e-book

NOTE TO READERS

This is an unofficial summary & analysis of *The Dichotomy of Leadership: Balancing the Challenges of Extreme Ownership* by Jocko Willink and Leif Babin. This summary is designed to enrich your reading experience.

CONTENTS

"When a leader takes too much ownership, there is no ownership left for the team or subordinate leaders to take. So the team loses initiative, they lose momentum, they won't make any decision, they just sit around and wait to be told what to do."

—JOCKO WILLINK, *The Dichotomy of Leadership: Balancing the Challenges of Extreme Ownership to Lead and Win*

INTRODUCTION

THIS BOOK IS WRITTEN by Leif Babin and Jocko Willink, two former US Navy SEALs who served combat tours in Iraq and now run a successful consulting firm specializing in leadership development. Each chapter begins with a story extracted from either their SEAL training or their combat experiences that illustrates particular leadership challenges, concepts, and solutions, which are then followed by a list of "Principles"—in this summary I list them as "Lessons."

Finally, the authors tie the concepts in the chapter to a practical business scenario that they have encountered in their career as consultants, showing how these principles also apply to leadership in the civilian world.

While there are three sections to this book and 12 chapters that cover a range of concepts, the overall lesson is that leaders must balance "Dichotomies of Leadership." Essentially, any good leadership trait or practice may become a liability if it is taken too far. Good leaders must recognize these dichotomies and strike a delicate balance between two extremes.

"If mistakes happen, effective leaders don't place blame on others. They take ownership of the mistakes, determine what went wrong, develop solutions to correct those mistakes and prevent them from happening again as they move forward."

—JOCKO WILLINK, *The Dichotomy of Leadership: Balancing the Challenges of Extreme Ownership to Lead and Win*

PART I

BALANCING PEOPLE

"So what does it take to win? Yes, you have to be determined. Yes, you have to be driven. Yes, you must have the unconquerable will to win. But to really win, to truly win at all cost, requires more flexibility, more creativity, more adaptability, more compromise, and more humility than most people ever realize. That is what it takes to win."

—JOCKO WILLINK, *The Dichotomy of Leadership: Balancing the Challenges of Extreme Ownership to Lead and Win*

CHAPTER 1

THE ULTIMATE DICHOTOMY

By Jocko Willink

THE AUTHOR RECOUNTS TALKING with a SEAL who had been shot in the leg and begged to stay in Ramadi, Iraq instead of being medically evacuated out of the unit. Afterward, Jocko thought of the wounded SEAL and the other men he led, describing them as being like his "friends," "brothers," and "children." He wanted to do anything possible to protect them, but his job and the mission demanded that he send them into extremely dangerous situations.

Jocko refers to this dilemma as "perhaps the ultimate Dichotomy of Leadership a combat leader must face." A leader must *care for troops while risking their lives*—and he knew that some of his men would die, given how many people were being killed in the area.

Unfortunately this dreaded situation became a reality during an operation in the south-central portion of Ramadi. As

Jocko watched drone footage of a lifeless body being carried out of a building after a battle, he was forced to control an array of emotions in order to continue doing his job. Later he would learn that the body was that of Navy SEAL Marc Lee.

The immensity of the grief felt by Jocko and Leif is indescribable. However, on top of that, Leif had to deal with the excruciating doubts about whether the course of action and the decisions he had taken as the platoon leader had been the correct ones. Jocko did his best to reassure him that he had made all the right calls—the only decision a good SEAL could have made—given the situation. SEALs, in both combat and training, face extreme risks and leaders must balance caring for their men while often putting their lives at risk in order to accomplish the mission. SEAL leaders know that risks can and should be mitigated—but they are also inevitable.

Nearly two months later, Jocko heard a radio call for the evacuation of multiple casualties during another mission. An Army battalion commander soon updated him that while three wounded SEALs would survive, a fourth was critically injured and likely would not make it. That fourth SEAL was Mike Monsoor, who was killed after diving on top of a grenade to protect his teammates.

Once back in the U.S, Jocko had a chance to have a conversation with the platoon leader of that mission, who felt responsible for Monsoor's death. To that platoon leader's surprise, Jocko agreed and stated that *they* were indeed responsible and explained that this responsibility is simply a fundamental part of being a leader.

Later, that same platoon leader was coincidentally offered Jocko's previous role. Given what this platoon leader had been through in Ramadi—intense combat including a fatality and several wounded—it would have been understandable if the man declined the position. Jocko conveyed to the platoon leader that he was in fact the most equipped and suited for the position. The SEAL decided to accept the role, viewing it as his duty.

LESSONS

- Leadership involves many dichotomies that necessitate striking a balance. Foremost among them is caring for your team while trying to achieve an objective. A leader must be close to his people but also be willing to carry out the tasks required of the role.

- War is the ultimate illustration of this dichotomy. A leader who is unable to prioritize critical, difficult choices won't make hard decisions and will ultimately and inevitably fail. This is also true of the opposite, a leader who takes unnecessary risks and haphazardly puts together plans that have no chance of success and will ultimately cost people's lives.

- This conflict carries less severe consequences in the civilian world, but it is still costly. Leaders who fail to establish an appropriate relationship and become too "chummy" with those they lead will not only have difficulty ordering individuals to do difficult things, broaching uncomfortable topics, or firing people when necessary, but they will quickly lose their respect and surrender any semblance of authority. On the other hand, a leader who does not have the welfare of his people at the forefront and puts them in environments rife with stress and discord, which can pose health hazards will lose all credibility as an apt or capable leader.

- Good leadership requires an adequate balance between the two extremes.

IN BUSINESS

Jocko recounts an interaction he had with a regional manager of a struggling mining company that had closed a mine in order to cut costs. The manager was intent on making sure that his employees be able to keep their jobs, either at his mine or being transferred to other mines. His point of view was that they were very hard-working individuals with a great deal of experience and skills, who could benefit the company by increasing production.

As Jocko listened during the coaching session with this manager, and as the manager grew more hostile and argumentative—even suggesting that Jocko, being an outsider, couldn't possibly understand the situation. To this, Jocko calmly and succinctly replied that although he wasn't in the mining industry, he fully well understood having to make difficult decisions under difficult and stressful circumstances. Jocko had only to relate a few examples of having had to make very difficult choices that risked the wellbeing of people he very much cared about to get through to the manager.

The SEAL explained the "burden of command" and the dichotomy of caring for his people while having to make decisions that could put them in harm's way. He also pointed out that by trying to save some jobs in a manner that was alienating senior leaders and decision makers, the manager was actually putting the jobs of other workers at risk—maybe even his own! This resonated with the manager, who admitted that if he didn't take the necessary action, corporate headquarters would either replace him with someone who would or shut down the operation.

Jocko explained to the manager that although true leadership does in fact mean taking care of your people and standing up for them, it also involves having the fortitude to take a necessary action that will allow the company to continue to function and the mission to be accomplished, despite its harshness. The manager finally understood and proceeded to lay off a number of the people he'd been trying to keep employed. This manager realized that harming the mission can have worse consequences than making a difficult but correct decision.

"Accountability is an important tool that leaders must utilize. However, it should not be the primary tool. It must be balanced with other leadership tools, such as making sure people understand the why, empowering subordinates, and trusting they will do the right thing without direct oversight because they fully understand the importance of doing so."

—**JOCKO WILLINK,** *The Dichotomy of Leadership: Balancing the Challenges of Extreme Ownership to Lead and Win*

CHAPTER 2

OWN IT ALL, BUT EMPOWER OTHERS

By Jocko Willink

A 2003 TOUR IN Fallujah, Iraq was the first true combat experience for Jocko and the SEALs he served with. He compensated for this inexperience with overly detailed planning and meticulous execution, but his efforts strayed into micromanagement—which precluded any of his junior leaders from taking ownership of any part or aspect of the plan. This became a bigger problem as the pace of the operations became faster. The issue came to a head on a day when the unit needed to plan many operations at once.

Jocko had no choice but to assign planning to his junior leaders and was pleasantly surprised when they rose to the challenge, took charge of the situation, and developed effective plans. From that point forward, his subordinates took on a lot more responsibility for missions while Jocko still took overall responsibility in adherence to his leadership philosophy of "Extreme Ownership."

Reflecting on the change, Jocko realized that his junior leaders hadn't previously taken ownership because he hadn't permitted it. He had micromanaged the team. Jocko enjoyed several new benefits from his newly discovered ability to delegate: He could now look at things strategically, coordinate mutually supportive missions between teams, improve maintenance of men and equipment, and better accomplish the overall mission assigned to his team.

Jocko also came to the conclusion that he had earlier failed to strike the balance between "Extreme Ownership" and "Decentralized Command" that is vital for any successful leader. He hadn't empowered his subordinates enough, but in other situations, he had failed in the other direction by taking *too little* ownership.

As an example, Jocko recounts a maritime operation before deployment to Iraq: The SEALs were working with boat crews to create a new way of intercepting a vessel at sea. He entrusted subordinate leaders to handle the details, however the result was less than ideal with the team accomplishing things late, doing fewer rehearsals than scheduled, and simply not preparing well enough.

Although Jocko had noticed these shortcomings, he failed to intervene at the opportune time when he would have had a chance to change the outcome of the first rehearsal. Several major issues occurred at the rehearsal: several individuals showed up late—a serious problem in a naval movement—in addition, the team also realized that they had forgotten a key piece of equipment. They improvised but fell further behind schedule.

During the mission debriefing, these issues were mentioned but lacked taking accountability for by the team. He called all junior leaders into his office and told them that their performance was unacceptable. Further, he advised them that they had one more chance to get things right or they were finished—he would be forced to take charge.

The talk was enough to reshape the team's attitude and execution, and this renewed excellence carried over into the subsequent deployment to Iraq.

LESSONS

■ There are two opposing methodologies in leadership: micromanagement and "hands-off."

■ Micromanagement results in leaders using up too much time involved in the minutiae of the planning or the processes during a project or a mission. This method simply cannot work. It stifles creativity and initiative; it limits a leader's production; it alienates junior leaders who don't get the chance to lead.

- **Solution**: A way to rectify this situation is by assigning teams an overall goal allowing them the freedom to develop plans and execute them. However, it is important that a leader then take the appropriate time and measures to monitor and assess progress, providing guidance, but not stepping in unless not doing so will result in disaster. Eventually, the subordinate leaders will be fully equipped to take ownership.

- The hands-off approach often results in a lack of direction and cohesion. Some teams exhibit poor coordination, teams and workers exceeding the scope and authority of their jobs, individuals focusing on tasks that don't support the mission, and too many people acting in leadership roles.

  - **Solution**: Teams need structure, clarity, and vision. It is up to the leader to set the expectations and give the necessary guidance to accomplish the objective. Doing so includes defining the mission and its purpose, the limits of each individual's role, and the chain of command.

- A leader must find a balance between these two styles.

Jocko conducted leadership training at a software company that was having issues with the roll-out of a new product. Though it had already been sold, this automotive software was not complete, it had to interface with several different car manufacturers and models, and no production-scale manufacturing process had been developed.

Otherwise, the rapidly growing company was in good shape, having established a good track record and high demand for its product. Plans were underway to tackle the above problems, and the company atmosphere was positive after Jocko's initial training session. On a subsequent visit, however, the mood had darkened, and company personnel were worried that the new product would not be completed on time.

The CEO's feeling was that this negative turn stemmed from the senior leaders and expressed his desire to have them go through some training sessions with Jocko. As a part of his assessment, Jocko sat through various daily meetings held by the CEO. He observed meetings that were far too long, far too detailed, and stacked on top of each other. The CEO was also working directly with engineers who were handling details of the project while complaining that his employees were not taking ownership.

Jocko conveyed to the CEO that his observations had revealed that he was taking the concept of Extreme Ownership too far.

He suggested that he should clearly set expectations, convey his vision, give his team leaders clear, concise directions, and lessen his oversight. The CEO needed to stop making every decision, providing all of the answers, and find the balance between Extreme Ownership and Decentralized Command. It worked, and the product was on target for launch within a few weeks.

CHAPTER 3

RESOLUTE, BUT NOT OVERBEARING

By Leif Babin

LEIF RECOUNTS A "FRIENDLY-FIRE" incident in Ramadi, Iraq: a U.S. tank was shooting at his team of SEALs and a Marine forward air controller. Thankfully, he was able to switch to the tank's radio frequency and tell them to cease fire—only possible because he'd learned a new communications protocol after arriving in Iraq.

SEALs used different radios than the Army and Marines and traditionally relied on a single radioman to handle communications. Jocko had ordered all of the SEALs to learn how to use and program all of these different radios. Although most of the troops had not embraced the task, Jocko was adamant that the team learn the skills before the next mission—or they weren't going.

Another dichotomy that leaders will have to learn to navigate is knowing when to enforce standards and be tough, and when to be more lenient. Going to one extreme or the other will carry serious consequences for a leader—too rigid too often and your people won't respect you; too lenient or too yielding and you'll get a similar result.

Leif reflected about times when he had been too lenient about maintaining standards, being too worried about overworking them. Other times, he had strayed into being too firm and micromanaging the team, which resulted in unnecessary problems and reduced initiative.

While training to deploy to Iraq, for example, the SEALS knew they would be working with Marines and soldiers who had rigid standards about the uniforms they wore; standards that were almost non-existent in SEAL teams. In particular, SEALs wore self-designed patches that featured funny sayings and unique logos representing the unit. Some patches were crude and unprofessional, but Leif was reluctant to enforce a uniform standard, as he thought it would hurt morale.

Jocko, however, believed that the patches could cause friction with the units the SEALs would be working with and insisted that they were removed. The SEALs complied with his order. However, Leif thought the unit should be allowed one specially-designed patch; one that wasn't offensive but would serve to instill pride in the team.

He helped design two patches in secret and gave them to everyone in the task force after they had arrived in Iraq. The

SEALS didn't wear them on base but put them on as they departed on a mission. A journalist embedded with the Army took pictures of the SEALs out on patrol, and the secret was revealed. A senior enlisted leader reacted furiously at the disobeyed order, and Leif assumed that Jocko would punish the SEALs. He didn't. In this case, he simply ignored the violation of an order.

Later, Jocko explained why he had chosen to let the issue go: Most importantly, it hadn't harmed anyone, and the patches represented the SEALs as a cohesive unit. Also, only one patch was being used; the other offensive patches had been put away; the patch helped unit morale; and, because the patches were hidden from him, he assumed that the SEALs weren't flaunting it in front of the troops who had more rigid uniform standards.

Jocko's decisions to enforce the crucial standard of SEALs knowing how to program radios but letting the uniform standard slide illustrate how to balance this dichotomy of leadership.

LESSONS

■ Leaders must avoid going to easy on their people while also avoiding the inverse. They must rigidly enforce standards about important things while letting relatively unimportant matters go. This balance is achieved by careful analysis and listening to the team.

- "Leadership Capital" is a term that indicates a leader has a limited amount of authority, built up over time, that must be budgeted and spent intelligently. Spending it on enforcing trivial rules is a waste.

- When a leader must spend capital on enforcing rigid standards, the leader must explain why doing so is important. Issuing an order based on incoherent rationale or just using position or rank as an explanation will garner resistance.

IN BUSINESS

While performing a leadership assessment of a company, Leif met with the executive vice president. The company was expanding beyond its local market and wanted to implement standardized procedures among its teams and divisions.

The leader mentioned that "discipline equals freedom," one of Jocko's favorite sayings. He argued that the employees needed more discipline, citing their use of cellphones during meetings. He had barred the use of the devices and enforced the standard by making subordinates turn them off and show him they were shut down. Predictably, this was not popular.

Leif explained that there may be reasons why calls were necessary during meetings, including pressing issues that could impact the company. He explained the concept of leadership capital and the dichotomy between being overbearing and lenient.

The EVP had also encountered resistance to new standards that were being put into place. Leif advised the executive that he needed to explain *why* the company was implementing the standards—and illustrate *how* they benefit the team. But the EVP didn't see why this was his role or problem; he believed he should just be able to lead from authority.

Leif explained that military discipline is different than the Hollywood version. Leaders must still explain the rationale for key orders and learn to ignore trivial disobedience and other small matters. The EVP, in turn, needed to spend his leadership capital more wisely by letting go of the cellphone policy and focusing on the broader initiative, while better communicating the reason for the latter.

The EVP began to understand the need to balance this dichotomy of leadership.

"With such variation in individuals on the team, the challenge for any leader was to raise the level of every member of the team so that they could perform at their absolute best. In order to do that, a leader must make it his or her personal mission to train, coach, and mentor members of the team so they perform to the highest standards—or at least the minimum standard. But there is a dichotomy in that goal: while a leader must do everything possible to help develop and improve the performance of individuals on the team, a leader must also understand when someone does not have what it takes to get the job done. When all avenues to help an individual get better are exhausted without success, then it is the leader's responsibility to fire that individual so he or she does not negatively impact the team."

—**JOCKO WILLINK,** *The Dichotomy of Leadership: Balancing the Challenges of Extreme Ownership to Lead and Win*

CHAPTER 4

WHEN TO MENTOR, WHEN TO FIRE

By Jocko Willink

JOCKO DISCUSSES THE MANY threats during his deployment to Ramadi; the complexity involved in how an individual performed in combat, and how this complexity left little time to be afraid. His SEALs worked as a team that seamlessly functioned "as a single organism."

He explains that it took training and time to achieve this competence. Individual SEALs come from a range of backgrounds and have a variety of personalities and skills, and it is the responsibility of a leader to maximize each person's potential. But a leader must also know when someone is not cut out for the job and fire them to benefit the team.

Firing people is not easy, especially within Jocko's SEAL unit. Hard training and shared experience made team members extremely close.

The unit conducted six months of intense training before deployment and some new SEALs struggled. Jocko observed underperformers and how his subordinate leaders handled them. As leaders should, they spent a great deal of time and effort mentoring the new SEALs. These efforts paid off and the individuals improved in the first phases of training. Unfortunately, one individual continued to struggle during a phase that involved practicing with real ammunition, and Leif expressed concerns about him deploying.

This man was becoming stressed under pressure and making poor decisions that could get team members killed in combat or training. Upon hearing about the issue, Jocko made sure the platoon leaders had done everything possible to coach the SEAL. They had, and Leif thought it was best to fire him—until he learned to do so meant they would be a man short during deployment. They resolved to try and find a less stressful role in which the new SEAL could contribute.

Jocko and Leif continued to observe the man and he continued to struggle, even in a reconnaissance training phase that involved less pressure. His low performance impacted the team and the leaders eventually resolved to fire him. This was a difficult, career-ending decision made harder by the fact that everyone liked the man. But leaders had to weigh their commitment to this man against their duty to the team.

The unit conducted a review board made up of various leaders who decided to remove him from the SEALs permanently. Although he didn't like the decision, he seemed relieved, and went on to have a good career elsewhere in the

Navy. The other new SEALs who had struggled, however, had been mentored and contributed to a successful deployment.

LESSONS

- The majority of poor performers require coaching instead of firing. Nevertheless, when coaching fails, leaders must make the difficult decision.

- Leaders must take responsibility for each person on their team; recognizing their strengths and weaknesses and using them in appropriate positions that create value for the team.

- Sometimes, some people just can't contribute, and they must be removed. This creates a dichotomy between caring for and coaching an individual and looking out for the best interests of the team.

- This dichotomy can also conflict with the concept of "Extreme Ownership," since leaders hold themselves responsible for an individual's performance. Putting a great deal of effort into mentoring a person who does not improve winds up taking resources and attention away from others on the team. Leaders must balance helping one individual with the needs of the team.

- Fire people only after you have made a concerted effort to mentor them without seeing the needed improvement.

Jocko advised a construction company tasked with building two condominium towers. One of the tower projects was lagging behind the other. One of the project managers attributed this to one of the superintendents who was not performing as well as his counterpart.

When the issue was brought up to the vice president, the VP pointed out that it was the project manager's responsibility to figure out a solution. The project manager stated that coaching was having no effect, to which Jocko responded by asking why then he was still the superintendent. The project manager explained that the man held knowledge that was crucial to the project.

Jocko and the VP instructed the project manager to take further steps to coach and counsel the superintendent, including doing it in writing, as due diligence requisite for documentation if firing became the necessary course of action. This formal warning would send a clear message to turn things around *and* legally protect the company in the event of termination.

It is important that leaders realize what a difficult decision it is to fire someone. Jocko explains that it is important to give someone who is struggling every opportunity to turn things around. You owe it not only to the individual, but you owe it to yourself to do everything in your power to coach, guide, and instruct a struggling member of your team or unit. If you know you have done that, you won't have doubts or question your decision.

As Jocko and the VP instructed the project manager, it dawned on the VP that just as it was the project manager's job to fix underperformance or fire the superintendent, it was also his responsibility to do the same with the project manager. The VP told the project manager to provide written counseling to the superintendent but also start searching for a potential replacement within the team.

Despite their efforts, the man showed no improvement and was consequently fired. Fortunately, the superintendent running the other tower helped to identify and coach a replacement, and the project rapidly improved.

"So as a leader it is critical to balance the strict discipline of standard procedures with the freedom to adapt, adjust, and manoeuvre to do what is best to support the overarching commander's intent and achieve victory. For leaders, in combat, business, and life, be disciplined, but not rigid."

—**JOCKO WILLINK,** *The Dichotomy of Leadership: Balancing the Challenges of Extreme Ownership to Lead and Win*

PART II

BALANCING THE MISSION

"Instead of focusing on one individual, leaders must remember that there is a team—and that the performance of the team trumps the performance of a single individual. Instead of continuing to invest in one subpar performer, once a concerted effort has been made to coach and train that individual to no avail, the leader must remove the individual."

—**JOCKO WILLINK,** *The Dichotomy of Leadership: Balancing the Challenges of Extreme Ownership to Lead and Win*

CHAPTER 5

TRAIN HARD,
BUT TRAIN SMART

By Leif Babin

LEIF RECOUNTS HOW A key leader was injured and taken out of commission during a firefight. The SEALs were pinned down and a leading petty officer (LPO) was the next person in command. The man seemed overwhelmed, however, and the team waited for direction as the enemy flanked their position.

Someone needed to step into a leadership role, gather the SEALs, and decide on a course of action to move the unit to a less precarious, more advantageous position. Fortunately, this was a training scenario in a mock urban environment. It illustrated that the SEALs needed to learn how to handle chaotic situations and step up when leaders were taken out of the fight.

Leif explains how rigorous standards in training prepared his unit for deployment to Iraq, as well as how both he and

Jocko went on to apply those lessons in later assignments throughout their careers. Post deployment Jocko took over a training unit and focused on leadership development, having learned that leaders had been the crucial element of success during the combat operations he'd been involved in. He designed training exercises that put immense pressure on leaders at all levels to teach them how to react when unforeseen situations arise.

After his deployment, Leif also served as an instructor, teaching junior officers who had just completed the SEAL selection process, and later as an operations officer in a SEAL platoon. In these positions, he passed on leadership lessons learned in combat.

While in their respective roles, both Leif and Jocko observed and assessed training exercises that realistically simulated the types of situations that arise during combat. In one of those exercises, a particularly good leader was performing exceptionally well and Leif and Jocko decided to take him out of the simulation to force the other SEALs to react. Unfortunately, no one stepped up to take charge. The key leader was reinserted in order to illustrate the positive impact his presence would have. The rest of the students learned the importance of the elements of leadership the key leader had displayed and that they needed to emulate them.

In both combat and training, leadership was the most important element. To develop this skill, instructors had to strike a balance between training that overwhelmed participants and scenarios that challenged them. Leif describes going through a previous training exercise in which the instructors set up the trainees to get slaughtered, overwhelming them with a no-win situation; he explained that the value of the training was compromised by the fact that success was impossible. Leif writes that good training must be difficult but achievable for it to impart valuable lessons.

Some SEALs did not embrace hard training, specifically complaining about scenarios being too difficult compared to real-world scenarios. These individuals argued that the trainers were much more skilled than the enemies SEALs would face in combat. Leif's stance—as is that of many combat tested veterans—is that training must be designed and engineered to prepare individuals for the unpredictability and incalculable nature of combat missions; and a critical habit to adopt is to **never** underestimate the enemy. And much like the instructors, the real enemy in Iraq did not follow the standard rules used by the SEALs in combat.

Some instructors failed to adequately push their teams during training—inaccurately assessing subpar performance, allowing shortcuts, and overlooking problems for fear of being disliked or seeming unsupportive. Those who didn't enforce high standards wound up with inferior teams compared to those who did.

The effective leaders knew they needed to implement difficult scenarios and enforce very high standards—ensuring individuals were equipped to take on greater responsibility when necessary—but also knew how and when to back off to make sure the instruction was valuable. And the strategic goal of the training was always the long-term success of the team.

LESSONS

- Every successful team routinely implements difficult training. Good training challenges people to do uncomfortable things and allows them to learn from errors.

- Leaders must push individuals out of their comfort zone as long as they use realistic scenarios that impart vital lessons.

- Instruction needs to be realistic; it must involve scenarios that may happen in the real world, and role-playing and rehearsals should be a component.

- Training must cover fundamental concepts—basic skills and procedures that will have common use— before covering any advanced elements.

- Repetition is key to effective training. Continuous instruction develops lasting skills, but the lessons of individual sessions can be lost over time.

- Leaders must take responsibility for creating effective training programs and employ the most suitable leaders to conduct them.

Leif was consulting at a company that was experiencing excessively rapid growth, which was resulting in very inexperienced frontline personnel being thrust into leadership roles with an overwhelming amount of responsibility. Leif communicated to the company that the most efficient solution would be a leadership training and development program. Senior leaders expressed their skepticism stating that training couldn't reflect real-world experience.

Leaf easily countered this argument illustrating how SEALs who had never been to combat were fully prepared and equipped to successfully carry out combat missions in Iraq having been properly trained. He specified how training had prepared one SEAL, in particular, to perform exceptionally well as a platoon commander in his first ever firefight when a group of SEALs, Iraqi, and American soldiers were pinned down, this man quickly took initiative to flank the enemy and force them to retreat.

Leif explained that it was the mid-level leaders' responsibility to develop a training program for their people that would accurately simulate real-world scenarios and situations and show them how to react. They had the frontline experience and appreciation of the problem that the company's top executives lacked.

He advised them to develop role-playing scenarios and evaluate the trainees' performance. Several managers took the lead in developing the program but when Leif checked in several weeks later, he learned that there was resistance to its implementation.

The issue was identified: the first trainer had overwhelmed the trainees with information and acted harshly when they failed to learn it quickly. Leif stressed that although creating a training program was crucial, possibly more important was choosing the right person to carry it out. The key is in finding the balance between appropriately challenging and difficult and effectively instructive.

CHAPTER 6

AGGRESSIVE, NOT RECKLESS

By Jocko Willink

JOCKO DESCRIBES HOW ONE of his sniper teams became engaged in a firefight—and he didn't know what was going on. Nevertheless, as the ground force commander, his bias was to be aggressive and take action.

The mission was to clear a market and village near Ramadi, Iraq that was known to be a source of enemy attacks. SEAL sniper teams had entered first to conduct reconnaissance and set up to then provide security for the main force to make an assault.

Jocko and the rest of the assault force readied to move into the village at a combat outpost (COP). He went over plans and procedures with the leaders of the Army unit while everyone listened to radio traffic describing what was going on in the area. They learned that another allied unit was conducting an operation in the same area—and that they might be wearing local, nonmilitary clothing. This presented a major challenge, as the SEALs and soldiers would not be able to tell friend from enemy.

The SEAL team that had already entered the village soon reported that they saw a group of armed military-age males. Jocko told the overwatch commander to avoid firing on them unless they saw them commit a "hostile act," which was an unusual order. Jocko explained that friendly forces might be wearing local clothes. This made a combat scenario that was inherently confusing even more chaotic.

Then the firefight started, and Jocko could not get an update on what was happening. Despite this uncertainty, he stuck to the original plan and made the decision to carry out the assault on the village since the overwatch team was engaged. The overwatch team had fought off a team of insurgents preparing to attack, and the assault force successfully cleared and searched the village, capturing weapons and suspected insurgents.

This illustrates how SEALs are trained to have a bias for action; to be aggressive by default. But this presents a dichotomy of leadership because aggression should be balanced with caution when situations call for restraint.

The US Army brigade commander asked the SEALs to conduct another mission to take out insurgents who fired mortars from a rural area north of Ramadi. The insurgents had placed improvised explosive devices (IEDs) to protect the location. The SEALs evaluated the potential mission but determined that, despite their bias for action, it would not be a smart move.

There was no pattern to where mortar attacks originated from, the SEALs would be exposed entering the area, and receiving support would be difficult, given that there was only one entry point safeguarded by IEDs.

The SEALs and the brigade commander decided against the mission, balancing aggression with caution and risk with reward.

LESSONS

- Aggression is not a description of emotional conduct or interactions, such as yelling at others (which is counterproductive). It describes being proactive about solving problems and taking action to fulfill the mission.

- Leaders must solve problems aggressively. Allowing bad situations or issues to continue and become worse is a lack of leadership. By nature, a leader should have a bias for being proactive and aggressive within the intent of the mission.

- Aggression must be balanced with careful evaluation and restraint when situations call for them. This means pausing to assess how a situation unfolds before taking appropriate action. It is also important to consider advice from others.

- Leaders who fail to navigate this dichotomy of leadership and always respond with aggression are reckless.

- Jocko describes "the disease of victory" as a source of recklessness. This happens when a team succeeds and becomes overconfident. Successful leaders and teams must avoid complacency and *always* critically analyze a situation.

IN BUSINESS

Jocko recounts advising a CEO who had just purchased a small business that she intended to grow rapidly. Although her team was quickly acquiring customers, they still faced several challenges, including a lack of capital, numerous sales leads with low conversion rates, and lag time between receiving orders and payment. She also had plans to move the company to a new and expensive location. Her strategy and leadership attitude were aggressive, which Jocko liked.

Upon further thought and reflection, Jocko realized that he had been too enthusiastic in his approval of her strategy. He asked her to table any major decisions before they could conduct a financial review of the business and its plans. He consciously dialed back his enthusiasm to analytically review the numbers gathered by the CEO and her team.

The numbers showed a bottom line that might be achievable. But Jocko soon recognized that the projections were based on "stretch" sales goals—they could only be achieved by an expanded sales force that hadn't yet been hired. Given the operating capital on hand, this course of action could be reckless. Jocko explained that the CEO needed to focus on mitigating risk as aggressively as she did with expanding her company. He advised her to create a more cautious plan that included benchmarks and contingency plans depending on how the company was doing at each stage.

Jocko, the CEO, and her team created a new plan that eliminated some costs, slowed the growth of overhead, and based growth targets on performance. The CEO was still aggressive but balanced this with careful analysis. And she channeled her aggression into a direction that the company needed: risk mitigation instead of just rapid growth.

"A leader must care about the troops, but at the same time the leader must complete the mission, and in doing so there will be risk and sometimes unavoidable consequences to the troops."

—**JOCKO WILLINK,** *The Dichotomy of Leadership: Balancing the Challenges of Extreme Ownership to Lead and Win*

CHAPTER 7

DISCIPLINED, NOT RIGID

By Jocko Willink

JOCKO DESCRIBES THE FIRST time he was shot at while leading a SEAL platoon on his first combat deployment to Baghdad. While driving as a convoy of unarmored Humvees, they took fire from an unknown source resulting in one of the SEALs being lightly injured. When they arrived at a combat outpost, as the team assessed the injury, they began to take fire once again from an location and source. Unfortunately, they had driven past a set of large barriers that would protect them from the bullets. Jocko and the team became a bit disoriented and confused.

To solve the problem, Jocko defaulted to the standard operating procedures (SOPs) that SEALs learn in training. Jocko issued a series of commands that were repeated by each member of the team:

■ He identified the direction of the fire,

■ faced their weapons toward it,

■ and ordered the SEALs to move back toward the cover of the barriers.

This brief experience taught him how the disciplined application of SOPs enabled quick communication and effective action in a chaotic situation.

In other situations, however, Jocko observed how SOPs could hinder success. Later, as the commander of a task unit slated to deploy to Ramadi, he noted that one of his platoons was falling behind during land warfare training.

In land warfare training SEALs learn to patrol and react to enemy contact while using live rounds. It involves learning a series of commands and actions like the ones Jocko had previously used during his first firefight. Since actual rounds are used, it's usually important for SEALs to strictly adhere to the SOPs to ensure safety.

Initially all was well, but once the SEALs began doing this training in complex terrain—with ridges, depressions, etc.— one of the platoons began to react too slowly. Jocko decided to watch the platoon leader and see what was causing the issue. He soon figured out that the otherwise competent platoon commander was following the standard operating procedures too closely. If an SOP called for him to move to a certain spot based on his place in the formation, he moved to exactly that spot.

The problem with this strict adherence to SOPs was that he was the leader. Leaders must always maintain situational awareness to effectively guide their team, and a procedure that put this man in a place that blocked mobility and awareness made him ineffective. Jocko coached the platoon leader—in real-time, during an exercise—on how to adapt the SOPs to ensure that he could still move freely, see what was going on, and make the right decisions.

This leader's skill increased by learning a simple lesson: disciplined SOPs can and should be adaptable to the circumstances of the situation.

LESSONS

- Discipline is an essential characteristic of successful teams; Jocko and Leif stressed the concept that "Discipline Equals Freedom" in their previous book. Standard operating procedures and processes that are learned and repeated free up team members to spend creative energy on solving unique problems that aren't addressed by these methods.

- Inflexible adherence to and enforcement of SOPs stops team members from thinking critically, assessing situations, and taking initiative.

- Jocko advises striking a balance between a disciplined approach and "common sense:" Leaders must have the capability to analyze a situation and determine if team members need to change things up with a novel solution or adapt the SOPs.

IN BUSINESS

An otherwise-successful company was experiencing fewer sales for several months in a row, and Jocko spoke with the VP of sales to identify the problem. The VP explained that the company had introduced new, more stringent procedures for sales—new scripts and pricing, an increase in the requisite number of sales calls, as well as monitoring of those calls—to proactively improve a seasonally slow period. The new procedures were then tightened even further when they failed to yield the desired result.

Jocko consulted with some of the company's regional sales managers. They couldn't identify exactly why sales were down but speculated that new products or features might be a solution. He then spoke to the actual salespeople and observed their calls. Despite extremely polished scripts and deliveries, they closed very few deals. One member of the salesforce explained that the scripts were too perfect. He elaborated that the new procedures precluded the ability to make a human connection with prospects.

In addition, the tightened pricing model took away the salespeople's ability to offer deals that might close a sale, and the higher number of calls they needed to make incentivized them to move on to another call.

Jocko explained to the VP that overly aggressive, disciplined execution of procedures and not enough flexibility was costing them sales. The company adapted the procedures to allow the salespeople flexibility to spend more time on a call when needed, as well as the ability to offer discounts when it was advantageous to do so. Coupled with newly implemented sales training, the changes had a positive result and the company's sales increased.

"If you are more concerned for yourself than the people that work for you, you will ultimately lose. But if you put the team first, and make your true goal—not your own success—but the success of your team and their mission... If you, as a leader, put others above yourself... If you care for your team first and foremost... then you will absolutely win. That's what leadership is; the pure goal and righteous intent of putting your people and the mission ahead of yourself."

—JOCKO WILLINK, *The Dichotomy of Leadership: Balancing the Challenges of Extreme Ownership to Lead and Win*

CHAPTER 8

HOLD PEOPLE ACCOUNTABLE, BUT DON'T HOLD THEIR HANDS

By Jocko Willink

JOCKO DESCRIBES HOW THE SEALs broke out of an ambush in Iraq, and how this had become routine. The SEALs had been easily outperforming poorly trained enemies in missions to kill or capture insurgents. Straightforward, well-honed tactics and procedures developed in training were helping them dominate the insurgents. As a result, the SEALs became very confident and more aggressive in executing missions, and they adapted their plans and what they carried based on what was useful.

One adaption included leaving behind items that they felt didn't have a purpose and would cut down weight so the SEALs could move faster. Unfortunately, the confidence and the weight-saving measures were taken too far. Jocko noticed that several SEALs had removed the rear bulletproof plates from

47

their vests. Their theory was that it cut weight, and the SEALs didn't plan on putting their back to the enemy.

There was an inspection before each mission but Jocko and his subordinate leaders did not have the time to look over everyone's gear every time they went on a mission to ensure they had all the equipment they should. He needed to find a way to make sure everyone adhered to the mandates without having to verify.

Before going out on one mission, Jocko instructed everyone to put in their backplates. Afterward, he explained to his men that overconfidence could be very costly. He stated that it would be impossible to always know the enemy's position—it could be to their rear. He further expounded that any gains they made by cutting the weight of their back-plates would be greatly diminished by having to care for a fellow SEAL if he were shot in the back.

Explaining "why" they needed to think through what equipment was vital was more effective with Jocko's team than handholding and carrying out inspections. It empowered individuals to take responsibility and hold *themselves* accountable.

■ Oversight and accountability must be balanced with other ways to motivate subordinates to do something: explaining the rationale, getting them to engage with the course of action, and having faith that they will do so.

■ Detailed oversight can work, and it is the simplest method to ensure something gets done. But leaders do not have the time to conduct it without sacrificing attention that needs to be placed elsewhere. Once a team hits a certain size, it's not only impossible to oversee everything but the leader wastes time that could be spent on strategy and managing relationships.

■ Leaders must still hold people accountable, and extreme accountability may be applied when an individual is underperforming. But eventually, a leader must trust individuals to execute without supervision.

■ Accountability must be balanced with instruction and empowerment.

Jocko was consulting for a company that was using a new software program to track how one of their products was used by customers. The software helped technicians assess which products were installed, to spot problems, and to provide metrics to the sales team before they solicited these customers for additional services.

The company's national operations manager had reported that despite the various steps taken to incentivize technicians to utilize the software, they were not complying. This was causing problems for the personnel interfacing with the customers—they had no knowledge of issues that may have arisen or any context for what had been done for that customer.

Investigation into the matter revealed to jocko that, according to regional managers, the time it took to fill out the information took time away from getting jobs done, which meant a net loss based on the compensation structure. Team leaders explained that they were too busy managing complex schedules and customer service issues to properly ensure that the software was used. Technicians said that the process took way too long due to usability issues, including a lack of multiple-choice answers and poor cell reception causing timely page loads. Notably, Jocko also found out that the technicians had no idea how or why the data was valuable.

Jocko reported these findings to the national operations manager along with some courses of action: simplify the software based on ongoing feedback and explain why using the software benefited the company, their fellow employees, *as well as* the technicians themselves. Jocko outlined a series of reasons that ultimately explained how its use would end up providing more customers, pay, and job opportunities for the technicians. The leadership team created a presentation that outlined this rationale and developed a program that used frontline feedback to revise the software.

Leadership would still check on the software's use. But individuals were expected to perform and hold themselves accountable as they now understood the overall impact.

"Getting angry at others is ineffective, losing temper is a sign of weakness. The aggression that wins in the battlefield, in business or in life is not directed towards people, but towards solving problems, achieving goals and accomplishing the mission."

—JOCKO WILLINK, *The Dichotomy of Leadership: Balancing the Challenges of Extreme Ownership to Lead and Win*

PART III

BALANCING YOURSELF

"If you care for your team first an utmost, then you will absolutely win. That is the goal. To place your men and the mission ahead of yourself. That is how a leader can truly win at all costs."

—**JOCKO WILLINK,** *The Dichotomy of Leadership: Balancing the Challenges of Extreme Ownership to Lead and Win*

CHAPTER 9

A LEADER
AND A FOLLOWER

By Leif Babin

LEIF DESCRIBES A PATROL comprised of almost 50 SEALs, Marines, and Iraqi soldiers that was supporting an Army battalion moving into an extremely violent neighborhood in Ramadi, Iraq. The insertion of his unit was conducted by boat along a river to avoid IEDs.

When the SEALs disembarked and quietly moved into the neighborhood, the battery on the lead man's rifle laser pointer died, which would make it hard to aim accurately at night. Leif told the SEAL to continue despite the disadvantage. Soon after, the point man froze when he spotted an armed insurgent about 75 feet away and moving toward the group.

Leif killed the insurgent and the team surged into nearby buildings. They soon saw IED clearance units enter the neighborhood and looked for a good overwatch position to provide cover for the main force. Leif and his point man, the experienced sniper Chris Kyle, disagreed on which building would make a better overwatch position. Leif, as the unit commander, had the authority to make a decision, however despite his doubts, he opted to defer to Kyle's expertise. Leif's decision proved to be the correct one. Kyle's choice of position enabled the SEALs to break up attacks from numerous insurgents and kill 21 of them. Leif's preferred building wouldn't have allowed the same capability to break up the attacks.

A leader must know when and be willing to follow if the situation calls for it.

Leif explains that he failed to wisely follow others as a leader numerous times in his career. Each failure diminished the trust and confidence his men placed on him.

One example Leif relates is when his platoon had conducted a training operation where the SEALs practiced boarding and taking ships at sea. Confusion ensued while conducting drills, as the team members used a variety of different terms to execute actions. Leif instructed them to use the terms he was familiar with but the senior enlisted SEAL who was present—a petty officer—disagreed, arguing that his method was better.

Leif ended the argument by pulling rank, but immediately regretted doing so. Later, he apologized to the petty officer for the way he had handled it, and the petty officer apologized in return for debating in front of the men. Upon reflection, Leif decided that if he had adopted the petty officer's suggestion, it would have strengthened his status as a leader by showing a willingness to not only learn from, but also to trust and follow more experienced subordinates.

LESSONS

- Leaders need to follow as well as lead. This involves deferring to others who have more experience as well as those with good ideas or specialized knowledge.

- Credit is irrelevant to a good leader, but they inevitably receive it if the team is successful. The leader should communicate and distribute this credit to the team.

- Subordinates should be encouraged to provide input when new perspectives may lead to success.

- Leaders should be good followers of *their* leaders. While a leader may provide alternative ideas to superiors, they must also earnestly execute a senior's decision, even if they don't agree with it. Obvious exceptions are when a decision is unethical, immoral, illegal, or otherwise poses an unacceptable risk.

- Being a good follower may be a challenge for aggressive leaders who work for individuals who are not as skilled and competent—but not doing it will undermine the hierarchy of the organization. It also creates a negative relationship with the chain of command

and makes senior leaders less likely to accept good input.

■ Leaders must learn to follow as well as lead, up and down the chain of command.

IN BUSINESS

Leif describes advising a corporate sales leader who needed help with leadership skills—specifically, getting along with his latest boss. The man stated that his boss was "unfairly harsh" and seemed to respond negatively when the sales leader received praise from a senior executive. The new boss also gave him unusually low scores on his annual performance review, causing an argument.

Leif quickly determined that the boss was likely intimidated by his subordinate's good performance. This was something Leif had dealt with frequently in his military career, and he notes that there are many poor leaders in all walks of life. In the past, he would often battle these types of leaders. But he eventually learned that there are smarter ways to handle these individuals that avoid conflict.

The sales leader wanted to protest the annual review—but Leif asked him if there was any scenario in which he would win that debate. The man quickly agreed that this would make things worse for him and his team. Leif explained that the sales leader was not living up to his mandate to be a good follower—which equates to failing as a leader.

Leif then challenged the sales manager on whether there were potential areas of improvement in his team.

The sales leader realized that some of the criticisms in the negative review had been fair assessments. Leif then instructed the man to take ownership of his failure as a follower and accept the negative review, followed by outlining—and executing—a plan for improvement.

Finally, Leif explained that a good leader strives to have a similarly positive relationship with every boss—good or bad—because it contributes to trust, success, and mission accomplishment.

"Don't try to plan for every contingency. Doing so will only overburden you and weigh you down so that you cannot quickly maneuver."

—**JOCKO WILLINK,** *The Dichotomy of Leadership: Balancing the Challenges of Extreme Ownership to Lead and Win*

CHAPTER 10

PLAN, BUT DON'T OVERPLAN

By Leif Babin

LEIF OVERPACKED EQUIPMENT DURING his first mission in Ramadi, Iraq. He took extra magazines, grenades, tracer rounds, batteries, water, and food—to be prepared for "every contingency imaginable." The weight quickly became a problem when he tried to execute the "cover and move" Maneuver. This involved one team sprinting down a whole city block while covered by another team. Leif endured, but the fatigue compromised his ability to lead effectively.

Leif adapted on the next mission, and this example reinforced the need to balance *over*planning for contingencies with *appropriate* planning—a lesson that applies to both individuals and teams.

During training, Jocko had advised Leif to plan for assaulting buildings with fewer men to avoid confusion within a structure. Leif had thought that having more shooters was better, but soon appreciated the wisdom of this training when carrying out missions in combat. Too many people inside a target added to the chaos, and teams with fewer men could execute with more flexibility.

He also learned that this maxim applies to plotting out every detail of a mission; the execution of these missions never goes exactly according to plan, and adaptability is required.

As with all of the elements Jocko and Leif mention in the book, this is a dichotomy that must be balanced. Contingency planning is necessary and useful. But plans must be pragmatic. They cannot account for every contingency, and teams must not be paralyzed by fear while taking necessary risks.

Jocko and Leif's unit had received criticism for taking too many risks during the deployment to Ramadi. But many critics weren't aware of some of the proposed missions that the unit turned down—including one support mission requested by another special operations unit. When Leif reviewed the plan, he decided that it was too aggressive and failed to plan for likely contingencies, such as the loss of a vehicle to a roadside bomb or the possibility that the planned route was blocked.

Leif confirmed that the plan was bad with a US Army National Guard company commander who had 15 months of experience in the area. The soldier told Leif that the special operations team would quickly hit an IED and get people injured. He related this feedback to the special operations unit's commander, but the man discounted the advice—despite the experience of the National Guard unit—and refused to plan for this contingency.

Leif refused the request for his SEALs to participate in the operation, but the other unit executed it anyway. As predicted, they quickly hit an IED, several individuals were injured, and the mission failed.

LESSONS

- Robust planning that accounts for likely contingencies is necessary to minimize risk and increase the odds of success. This applies equally to combat and business operations.

- Leaders must balance smart contingency planning with trying to account for every conceivable risk. Overplanning creates its own set of problems including needless complexity. Leaders must only plan for the most likely scenarios; about 3–4 contingencies and a worst-case scenario.

- *Under*planning is also a risk. Ignoring likely risks and not having contingencies in place can easily lead to failure. This is usually a symptom of overconfidence and complacency that result from "success sickness."

- Leaders must understand the dichotomy between underplanning and overplanning by closely evaluating risks and deciding which of them must be accounted for.

IN BUSINESS

Jocko and Leif implemented a Leadership Development and Alignment Program for a company's mid-level managers and senior executives. The company had been enormously successful, recently acquired a great deal of capital, and planned to expand.

The CEO and much of the senior leadership were very confident—but the COO had concerns about a failure to plan for contingencies. Chief among his worries were growing in different areas simultaneously and the significant expense of hiring more staff and leasing new space. The COO believed that market downturns or unforeseen production problems could cripple the effort. And if both of the two new subsidiaries failed, the situation might end the company itself.

The COO thought that the company should launch one subsidiary at a time—launching the second after the first succeeded—and not lock the organization into leasing as much new office space and hiring as many new people. Jocko and Leif thought the man's concerns seemed reasonable and that contingency planning was required.

They explained various things the SEALs did to plan contingencies that mitigated likely risks during combat operations. They also detailed how they attempted to "humble" SEAL leaders during training by setting up scenarios where things went wrong.

In one training scenario, the trainers would lure the unit into a trap—an assault on a fortified position in a hallway—until the SEAL leader invariably got much of the team "killed." The trainers would then intercede and point out to the leader that he needed a contingency plan; in this case, attacking the position from a different direction. These contingency plans work better when they are developed *before* a mission, so the team reacts quicker and more effectively.

They advised the COO to develop a report for senior leadership that outlined the major risks to the company's new venture—while detailing contingency plans to address these risks.

"Good leaders are rare; bad leaders are common."

—JOCKO WILLINK, *The Dichotomy of Leadership:*
Balancing the Challenges of Extreme Ownership to
Lead and Win

CHAPTER 11

HUMBLE, NOT PASSIVE

By Leif Babin

LEIF WAS ROUTINELY HUMBLED by what he experienced in Ramadi; whether it was being surprised by a new insurgent tactic or realizing a need to further decentralize command, have greater coordination with other forces, or issue clearer orders. He writes that the constant dangers in Ramadi forced the SEALs to "be humble or get humbled."

After arriving back at base after a mission, Leif was informed that higher leadership wanted to take one of his senior non-commissioned officers—one of only two of these critical leaders—to participate in a special, high-profile mission. The request came not just from his task force's immediate superiors but a level *above them*.

Leif's immediate reaction was resistance; an instinct to protect his people and key resources. But he also recognized that good leaders are humble enough to dispassionately review a given situation and prioritize the needs of the overall mission, not simply their unit. Leaders must support the chain of command and may need to share resources because they do not always see the broader strategic picture.

But higher leadership did not always understand how strategic decisions impacted the tactical picture. They didn't have the perspective and experience of the personnel who were executing missions in a given area. And sometimes, leaders must educate their leaders on these realities. They must push back on directives that will be detrimental to mission success.

After carefully reviewing the impact of losing this member of his team, Leif said he could not comply with the request, citing "potentially deadly consequences." Jocko communicated these concerns to higher leadership and an alternate arrangement was made.

Leif also provides another example of pushing back: higher leadership had mandated a ratio of seven Iraqi soldiers for every U.S. special operator on a mission. This was done to force reluctant units to train the Iraqis, which was a larger strategic goal. But the SEALs in Ramadi had very few Iraqi soldiers to work with, and this ratio would have forced units to deploy with only two or three Americans—a very risky proposition. Jocko and Leif successfully communicated why they could not comply with this rule.

Leif explains that pushing back is sometimes necessary, but it should be rare. Frequently bucking orders or requests hurts the leader's and the team's relationship with senior leadership, and loses them credibility. If this credibility is lost, the team loses the ability to push back on truly important things.

His unit had successfully pushed back in those instances because they had maintained this credibility with higher leadership. The SEALs consistently complied with numerous directives—some of which were difficult or didn't seem important—and this built trust. The key to doing it was having humility, a characteristic that also established trust with the conventional units the SEALs worked with.

Conventional units sometimes had bad experiences with special operations forces who acted arrogantly and refused to collaborate. Jocko and Leif's unit took the opposite approach: they treated the soldiers with respect, collaborated extensively, and even adhered to the same uniform and grooming standards to fit in. Even small gestures, such as pitching in to help with moving sandbags after a long mission, had an outsized impact on showing humility and gaining respect.

These efforts solidified a mutually beneficial relationship. The SEALs and soldiers supported each other, often at great personal risk to themselves.

LESSONS

■ Jocko and Leif define humility as "the most important quality in a leader." A lack of it and an inability to accept and learn from errors was the main reason they fired SEAL leaders. It is also vital in the business world.

■ Humility can be taken to the extreme and stray into passivity, however. Sometimes, leaders must resist bad orders and communicate issues with their superiors for the good of the team and the success of the mission.

■ Accomplishing this balance is helped by simply knowing that this dichotomy exists, and it must be managed.

IN BUSINESS

Leif describes a leadership training session with a technology company. During the discussion phase, he opened up the floor for leaders to identify problems that weren't being solved. The CEO quickly brought up the team's failure to implement a new software solution. He expressed his frustration and a belief that the leaders were simply resistant to change.

Leif asked the room of leaders if they understood why the software was needed and received some nods but also silence. Leif suggested emphasizing the rationale for the program and the CEO re-explained the need to increase efficiency in tracking clients and projects, and to keep up with competitors who used better software than the company's current program.

Since the leaders seemed to understand the need, Leif asked why the solution wasn't being implemented. One leader explained that the software created significant new problems and then provided concrete examples. Another leader agreed with the negative assessment.

While these leaders claimed that they had attempted to communicate these issues, the CEO was surprised and concerned by the feedback. Leif concluded that these leaders had failed to push back clearly and effectively, and that they must be able to "lead up the chain of command" more effectively. The CEO had also failed to seek feedback, truly listen to his team, and investigate the issue.

This new understanding led the CEO to authorize the leaders to find a new software solution.

"There is no growth in the comfort zone."

—JOCKO WILLINK, *The Dichotomy of Leadership: Balancing the Challenges of Extreme Ownership to Lead and Win*

CHAPTER 12

FOCUSED, BUT DETACHED

By Leif Babin

LEIF DESCRIBES A MISSION to capture an insurgent from a house in Ramadi, Iraq. After a group of SEALs and Iraqi soldiers breached the front door with explosives, they lined up outside of a locked room. They were about to breach this door when the sound of gunfire echoed throughout the space. Leif and his team thought that the insurgent was shooting at them through the door, and they prepared to toss a grenade into the room to eliminate the threat.

Leif, however, thought that something was wrong so he stepped back from the group and looked around. He discovered that an Iraqi soldier had accidentally discharged his weapon; this was the source of the gunfire. He ordered a SEAL preparing the grenade to stand down and they breached the door normally. In the room, they found the unarmed insurgent with his wife and four small children. By stepping back and assessing the situation, the team captured the insurgent while avoiding horrific civilian casualties.

This was a good example of why leaders must detach themselves from immediate details to assess the overall picture.

Another example involved Leif's first mission to capture or kill an insurgent. The SEALs had to formulate a plan and file numerous documents to receive approval. Unfortunately, Leif spent most of a day working on approval and not enough time on the plan itself. He told Jocko that he didn't think his team would be ready in time, but Jocko told Leif that he was over-thinking things and to press ahead.

Jocko viewed this task from a strategic lens. He knew that it was important to start running missions as soon as possible to gain experience and show the value of the SEALs to other units. Leif refocused his attention on planning and briefing and they launched the mission. It was a success.

This illustrated a lesson that Jocko and Leif have stressed in their previous book: the need to "Prioritize and Execute." To do this, Leif had to detach himself somewhat from the planning details and trust his team.

As with every other aspect of leadership, a balance between detachment and focusing on details is necessary. Leif learned this lesson the hard way When after another mission, a radioman informed the team that he had lost a very import-ant piece of communications gear. This was a significant misstep because the equipment was highly classified, and there were numerous standard procedures in place to ensure that it was never lost.

Leif investigated the reason for the loss and found that his radioman had not followed the procedures. The incident was embarrassing and reflected poorly on the SEALs. And while Leif was angry with his men, he ultimately realized that it was his responsibility. He had become so detached—trusting his team to execute proper procedures—that he had failed to periodically supervise these details. The individual who lost the gear had been very reliable, but Leif had focused too little of his attention on checking basic accountabilities.

Leif and his team searched for the missing equipment but never found it. He resolved to avoid such an error in the future by balancing necessary detachment with attention to detail—in this case, periodically ensuring that proper procedures were being followed.

LESSONS

- Leaders must balance attention to detail with a detachment that allows them to see the bigger picture and lead effectively.

- This general principle also applies in business environments, and all leaders sometimes find it difficult to detach from details.

- Leaders must not detach so completely, however, that they don't understand what the details are or how and whether details are being implemented. Having this basic understanding and oversight enables leaders to support their team as it executes. Not having these elements can result in losing control of the team and the mission.

IN BUSINESS

Leif and Jocko's company, Echelon Front, was hired to conduct a leadership development program for a successful company; senior leaders realized that the organization needed formal training as it grew. Follow-up training sessions required these leaders to leave their office, which detached them from day-to-day activities and helped them achieve strategic focus.

During a training session with 15 senior leaders, one individual assessed that "modularization" of all activities was the key to success. Leif asked why this person had thought of this solution now, rather than the day before. The man responded that he had been so busy handling his daily accountabilities that he had not had the time or attention to consider it. Leif noted that simply stepping away for a day's training session had allowed this perspective, and explained how leaders on or off the battlefield need this detachment.

He cautioned, however, that balance must be achieved between detachment and appropriate supervision. He provided an example from SEAL training: he'd always been instructed to place himself at the end of a "train" of men during exercises where the team assaulted a target.

Jocko pointed out, however, that Leif couldn't tell what was happening at the front of the train—he should place himself in the middle. This advice taught Leif a lesson about adapting guidance to achieve better awareness.

He then advised the senior leaders how to apply this principle to their business. Leaders must detach to achieve perspective but also know what is going on to step in and solve problems.

Leif provided another example of a SEAL leader who was too detached during a training operation; the man stayed outside in a truck while his team assaulted a building, and thus had no idea that the unit was sustaining significant (simulated) casualties. Jocko and Leif asked the man what was happening, but he had no situational awareness. They advised him to move toward the team. The SEAL had learned the lesson that when things go wrong, a leader must be aware of it and take action to lead.

This lesson applies equally to business leadership. To succeed, individuals must handle this dichotomy between detachment and hands-on awareness and action.

OTHER BOOKS
BY CHRIS LAMBERTSEN

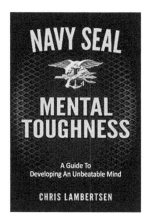

Navy SEAL Mental Toughness:
A Guide To Developing
An Unbeatable Mind

https://amzn.to/2xpb2JY

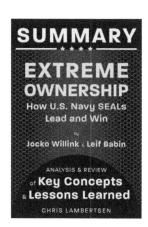

Summary of Extreme Ownership:
How US Navy SEALs Lead and Win
by Jocko Willink and Leif Babin

amazon.com/dp/0989822966

DO YOU HAVE A MINUTE TO HELP ME OUT?

Dear Reader,

Thank you for taking the time to read this summary of *The Dichotomy of Leadership: Balancing the Challenges of Extreme Ownership* by Jocko Willink and Leif Babin. I hope you found it useful, insightful and enjoyable.

If you have a minute, could you help me out by leaving a review on Amazon?

Your review is incredibly important to the success of this summary on Amazon. It only takes a few moments, and I would be deeply grateful for your support.

If you've never left a review before, it's super simple:

STEP 1: Type the following link in a browser:

https://amzn.to/3creV0m

STEP 2: Sign into Amazon if you aren't already signed in.

STEP 3: Choose your star rating and write a review. It doesn't have to be long, even a few words will do. The title is optional, so feel free to leave it blank.

Thank you for your help and support! It means a lot to me!

Best regards,
Chris Lambertsen

Made in the USA
Las Vegas, NV
19 September 2021